THE DAY LAID BARE

THE DAY LAID BARE

Kiwao Nomura

translated by Eric Selland

ISOBAR
PRESS

This translation first published in 2020 by

Isobar Press
Sakura 2-21-23-202, Setagaya-ku,
Tokyo 156-0053, Japan

&

14 Isokon Flats, Lawn Road,
London NW3 2XD, United Kingdom

https://isobarpress.com

ISBN 978-4-907359-32-4

ヌードな日 (*Nuudo na hi*) originally published by Shichosha
(Tokyo, 2011).

Cover photograph by Kiwao Nomura.

Contents

Introduction   7

The Day Laid Bare   13

Notes   75

Author & Translator   81

INTRODUCTION

Eric Selland

The Day Laid Bare by Nomura Kiwao[1] opens with a quote from Gherasim Luca, a Romanian surrealist poet who lived in Paris from 1952 till his death by suicide in 1994. The statement, 'There is no place left in this world for poets,' is something that Nomura can relate to. For Nomura himself, when he began writing this book, felt that poetry had lost its central role in Japanese culture.

Hence the book begins with a sense of crisis – a general cultural crisis. In fact, Nomura locates the very source of modern Japanese poetry in crisis – 'without crisis, there would be no modern Japanese poetry. This is true beginning with Hagiwara Sakutarō in 1916 and it is true for the postwar poets and those writing just after the end of the Shōwa Period'[2] (Nomura Kiwao, *Shi no Gaia wo Motomete*, [In Pursuit of Gaia in Poetry], 2008).

It is this feeling of cultural crisis and the sense that the poet has now become an outsider or exile from Japanese culture that is the original impetus of *The Day Laid Bare*, but then in the process of writing, the Great East Japan earthquake occurred, making this crisis something very real and very physical, affecting everyone in Japan. For many artists and intellectuals, the earthquake and the nuclear accident that followed seemed to be a sign of Japan's imminent collapse. This is where the poem becomes even more passionate, gaining in momentum and texture. The political begins to appear in the form of deeply ironic statements about Japan (using the English rather than the Japanese name for the country) suggesting the possibility of a post-colonial interpretation of Japan's status in relation to the U.S.

Certain key words are central to Nomura's poetic vocabulary: words like 'flesh', and 'parade'. The words 'roadblock' and 'parade', which name the various sections of the poem, have metaphoric meanings. Nomura doesn't like to say exactly what they mean in precise terms, but there is a range of meanings, or a field, which naturally forms around these key words, and which the reader gradually develops a feel for.

The parade is a metaphor for society, i.e. the world or the worldly. It is mostly negative. The pieces of flesh move along in the parade like a Felliniesque carnival, unaware and unconscious of themselves or the deeper meaning of existence. They are inhuman or subhuman – or sometimes 'all too human' (Nietzsche).

In contrast, the roadblock stops everything. The term, *bousaku* could also be translated as 'barricade', bringing an echo of the French Revolution. It also may be an allusion to Nomura's own past as a Leftist student during the protests against the renewal of the security treaty with the U.S. in 1970. The roadblock brings a halt to the parade of flesh and we are given a moment of contemplation – the poetic moment, which is the real heart of the poem. While the parade sections read more like fragmented descriptive prose with free verse interludes (and with an ample amount of irony and sarcasm), the roadblock sections are passionate and expressive, moving into the territory of not only the lyrical but something like Rimbaud's 'derangement of the senses.' This is Nomura's poetic ideal, one that stands in contrast to his academic learning in which knowledge and the rational are central. In a way, Nomura's Apollonian side must give way to the Dionysian in order to reach a deeper space, which is also the realm of the sacred. Nomura's method of composition is of some interest here. He types directly into the computer, composing spontaneously in something like a stream-of-consciousness approach to writing. Here is where the poem develops its momentum and its rhythm. Reading aloud in live performance or with music is an important activity for Nomura, and it is here where the spoken tone of the poem begins to make sense. Nomura does not lack that element of *écriture* or inter-subjectivity so important to many contemporary experimental writers, but there is a direct path open to the spoken. Voice – the actual voice (*nikusei*, the Japanese word for the natural voice – that is, without microphone or amplification – means literally 'flesh of voice') is yet another important word in Nomura's poetic vocabulary.

Nomura's major influences are largely French. First, René Char – whose complete poems he translated – and of course Rimbaud. He could almost be a European poet, but this does not make him less Japanese; Paris has in fact been the Mecca of Japanese artists and poets since the early twentieth century, hence the above is nothing unusual. The same can be said regarding his reliance on continental philosophy for the source of his ideas and poetics. This too is shared with other Japanese writers. What is unusual is the breadth of this knowledge. In fact, if we were to unpack each one of the words in Nomura's poetic vocabulary we would find a web of complex philosophical and poetic relationships. For instance, the word 'flesh' featured so prominently in this book derives from the thought of phenomenologist Merleau-Ponty and his attempts to map human perception.

Nomura has a very respectable list of Japanese influences as well, including the post-war poet Naka Tarō (1922–2014) and the important earlier poets Hagiwara Sakutarō (1886–1942) and Nishiwaki Junzaburō (1894–1982), both major figures in modern Japanese poetry during its formative years.[3] In particular, he shares the sense of poetic ecstasy, of the Dionysian, with Hagiwara.

Nomura has a sense of the Felliniesque. His poetry is filled with absurdities, humor, and even silliness. The absurd or silly tone is effected with the use of colloquial expressions, verb forms and tag phrases which are common in daily speech patterns. The problem for the translator lies not only in the fact that many of these expressions or grammatical forms are impossible to translate into English, but that even where translatable they simply do not work in the same way. Perhaps this is matter of cultural sensibility, but it is not easy in English to be silly and absurd, yet dead serious at the same time. This mixture of styles or modes of speech can make Nomura difficult to pin down, and it means that the translator is forced to make some hard choices. Translation in general is of course a highly complex, time-consuming and often frustrating process, but even in this context, translating Nomura is an extremely intensive, all-consuming activity. One has to give oneself to it body and soul. In a sense one is obliged to become a medium, allowing the soul of the poet, the spirit of the poetic process itself to enter one, and to re-enact the process of original poetic production. It is a process which at its end finds the translator himself transformed, perhaps even more so than language as such. And hopefully, the reader of the new work in translation will have been transformed as well.

NOTES

[1] Throughout this book names of Japanese people appear in Japanese order with the surname first, except in the case of the cover and the title page – where Nomura's name appears in the English order – and in mentions of Japanese writers or translators who publish primarily in English.

[2] The Shōwa Period ended in 1989.

[3] For Naka Tarō, see *Music: Selected Poems*, translated by Andrew Houwen and Chikako Nihei (Isobar Press, 2018); for Hagiwara Sakutarō see *Cat Town* (New York Review of Books, 2014) and *The Iceland* (New Directions, 2014), both translated by Hiroaki Sato; for Nishiwaki Junzaburō see *The Modern Fable* (Green Integer, 2007), translated by Hiroaki Sato, and *The Poetry and Poetics of Nishiwaki Junzaburō: Modernism in Translation* by Hosea Hirata (Princeton UP, 1993).

THE DAY LAID BARE

There is no place left in this world for poets.
— Gherasim Luca

PARADE 1

The day laid bare

Exposed

ROADBLOCK 1 *(Sand on Lips)*

When disquiet
With its as many as one hundred legs
Puts down roots all around me

Whose voice is this?

You have to go on with your own water
As far as that of which we cannot speak

With water?
All wet and shiny?
Losing all my color?

A distorted face appears
A monkey wrench for a neck
Sand
On lips

PARADE 2

The day laid bare

Go in pursuit of unknown flesh, of the disappeared
If not, you yourself will become a fugitive

Stripped to the bone

Ground of unraveling sutures
Remains of dissolved flesh
Awaken
Go, follow – give chase

It's a parade. **FIRST FLESH** arrives. Seems like a mere octopus, or something an octopus has on its exterior. It moves forward, spewing nonsense, but then, as it grows distant, it is revealed, revealing, no doubt, the human. Then it multiplies, from belly to belly, a fetus with only a head seen in perpetual motion.

Seen in perpetual motion

With **FIRST FLESH** in front, **SECOND FLESH** undulates. Go in pursuit of that wretched nerve center mimicking animated ashes

Because it is equal to the fate of the breast

All is laid bare
The stones give off a scent in the confusion (according to internet media rumors, there was a tattoo imprinted on the breast)

THIRD FLESH – of all things, masquerading as sand, or engulfed by sand, in either case, all that can be seen is sand, an enormous amount of sand, its sun-soaked, smug expanse.

All is laid bare
Attaboy!

'Two pages torn from the latest issue of a comic book, *Hunter x Hunter*'

FOURTH FLESH is working. For instance, when you are immersed in afternoon sleep in the eternity of water, that which multiplies into many fish gathers together and eats the history of your diseased skin, eats it all up nicely.

FIFTH FLESH is so smelly you could call it stench incarnate

All is laid bare
Like gum which has lost its flavor, I who am nothing more than myself

SIXTH FLESH is a hand shaking pom-poms all around. How ridiculous. It's not as if it's a cheer leader. It should probably be thrown off the field. It has the limitations of a crustacean.

SEVENTH FLESH is the shadow of flesh shimmering, giving birth to flesh though it is a mere shadow, raising its young in the hollow of an eye socket. Hold them in your arms when they're grown – you'll be covered in blood. Why? Are you saying live out the sullen remainder of your days as a monk?

Adenylic acid, guanylic acid

'While walking in the Western Market someone stumbled toward me, skin blackened as if they had attempted to burn themselves alive'

Like gum which has lost its flavor, I who am nothing more than myself

ROADBLOCK 2 *(Atomic Bomb Brick)*

Of course it's not as if
An atomic bomb brick
Came flying over nor is it the case that
I brought it home
Placed
Here right out of the blue
This suddenness continuing forever
Or something like that
An atomic bomb
Brick
Actually, a screenwriter friend
Came like the wind from Hiroshima to my house
And gave it to me as a gift
Taken
From the Calbee Foods warehouse
Formerly the Hiroshima military supply depot
Its pedigree noted on a piece of paper and again like the wind
He left
But how troublesome
I tried adding it to the objects arranged in the entryway but it
        just didn't fit
Then I moved it to the glass case in the living room
With the rock collection
But still it didn't fit
An atomic bomb
Brick
Wrested from the depths of the earth
A fragment, covered
With fine scars, a mysterious
Fragment
Or something like that
So I placed it on the palm of my hand

Nothing to do but gaze fixedly at it
And then music I'm sure it was
Music I heard coming from somewhere
In the bone at the bottom of the ear
A torrent of metallic blood
Colliding, crushing
Dissipating
The metallic
Rainbow squeaking, made to undulate severalfold
Or something like that

PARADE 3

Stripped to the bone

The day laid bare

No one can escape
And yet there are runaways, always runaways, everywhere – it is the real.

EIGHTH FLESH appears, in every respect its flattened figure a kind of zone – blood zone, knowledge zone, ground zone. Each zone separate, the gaps between their names which matter little are sewn up. A voice is heard from somewhere saying it's all gas so there's not much you can do.

'The collarbone snaps'

NINTH FLESH – one becomes mesmerized by its swimming around and around aimlessly. Said to have the ability to charm, those who have grown weary are warned against becoming so inactive they end up falling in with a plop, to float next to **NINTH FLESH**.

Cytidylic acid, thymidylic acid

In this way **FOURTH FLESH** and **SIXTH FLESH** run strictly parallel, competing in their hushed silence like cotton. Eventually they are surprised to find they have transformed into **NINTH FLESH**. Similarly, **SEVENTH FLESH** and **FIRST FLESH** collide, thereby forming **TENTH FLESH**, while **FIFTH FLESH** and **THIRD FLESH** merge to form **ELEVENTH FLESH**. Meanwhile **SECOND FLESH** and **EIGHTH FLESH** move along arm in arm, the perfectly harmonious couple, but of course, they produce nothing.

TWELFTH FLESH is blind, but it is of course specialized, and is a master at spewing out words, much more so than **FIRST FLESH**, but obviously it has no reproductive capacity. It is a disposable product.

Much like myself

If someone asks, it must be **THIRTEENTH FLESH**. The spirit just makes it in, but the two are at cross purposes. When the spirit tries to lie down the flesh stands up, and when the flesh needs to rest the spirit gets up, walks around in the arcade of bones and joints, and tries to go outside.

FOURTEENTH FLESH wears an expression of anger and indignation, so one must hasten to apologize or else one might get clobbered, or draw its profile using quick-drying ink

Or something to that effect

FIFTEENTH FLESH has discarded eyes and ears, even its beautiful legs, and has renounced mathematics, single-mindedly developing the meaning of its existence in a region inundated by sand, but the result is more like an eye socket laughing meaninglessly above a set of kneecaps, or nerves foaming up in order to dream.

SIXTEENTH FLESH is an old curmudgeon, gradually cozying up to the meaning of existence once he's found it. He opens his big mouth, which can only be described as like that of a comic book character, and gulps everything down at once.

With frightening speed
Actions take hold of the human

Blood drips
From the hands of people become like empty shells

Like testimony

To the here

And the now

ROADBLOCK 3 *(Oh la la Piece 'a Meat)*

Oh la la
Piece 'a meat

Jostled to the tips of its toes the nonperson
Heads toward the chaos of a foaming polar region

The nonperson laughs from its knees
While streets and more streets surge forth in a coma

The nonperson devours thighs
And the bruise of love floats there like a dirigible

The nonperson hurries towards a backside
While longing resounds like the roar of the sea

The nonperson swings its hips
And the structure of woman becoming water without end
 becomes visible

The nonperson shuts itself up inside its navel
Mother, soon a casket will dance in midair

The nonperson climbs up a back
And bones grow from the bed, flowers blooming from
 their tips

The nonperson scratches its belly
While the metallic grass demonstrates mental telepathy,
 making a mechanical noise

The nonperson raises a racket in the heart
Is that forested place the door to the other world that has begun
    to decay?

The nonperson sits on shoulders
That there is no end is a frightening rod I should think

The nonperson slits someone's throat
Only the freedom of being torn to pieces screams at the top of
    its voice

The nonperson runs through the mind at the last minute
It is the dazzling glare in which at any moment the skin is peeled
    away to reveal another head

Piece 'a meat
Oh la la

PARADE 4

Naked day

Neither relief nor comfort
All is friction and discord
A grating sound – loud, resounding

Go, follow – give chase

A parade it is. **SEVENTEENTH FLESH** comes into view. It is a string. Assuming there is a space which could be called something like the scheme of things, it is from this space the black string comes, wandering. Soon it stands transfixed like a wire, but thinking this is suspicious, you throw water on it for more ambiguity. Then it starts to dance like crazy.

EIGHTEENTH FLESH stands on its head till it dies, and this most likely due to minor problems. Or it turns into a spirit and spreads its wings, dreaming of its own future.

NINETEENTH FLESH, at one time covered in its entirety by one face, which now gradually disappears, or at least this is one way to describe it – those hollow eyes opening, their subtle twitching. Now even more so you think about this – what is this heaviness, like water pressure? Where does it come from, and how? Then the questions are revealed like the rounded prominence at the end of a bone.

Passing through hell
A broken piece of blue sky hovers
In the gloom
Hieroglyphs of insects fly past

TWENTIETH FLESH is sleepy, always sleepy. Hence it makes one feel there is some kind of depth or intelligence there, but of course there's not even a speck.

TWENTY-FIRST FLESH flies. If it did not, it would be in danger of being devoured by the fervid boundary of its own shadow.

TWENTY-SECOND FLESH speaks – 'If discovered by the female while still in the larval stage, the male is absorbed by the female and spends the rest of its life inside the small compartment of the womb.'

In this way, **EIGHTEENTH FLESH** fuses with **TWELFTH FLESH** and is brought into parallel with **ELEVENTH FLESH** and **FIFTEENTH FLESH**, while **TWENTY-FIRST FLESH** and **SEVENTEENTH FLESH** reach a point of torsion, entering a relationship of 'eat or be eaten' with **THIRTEENTH FLESH** and **NINETEENTH FLESH**.

At the frayed ends of the eyes
I was the range, the sphere, the limit …

Fear and trembling rises in the form of a tower
And then collapses

And again rises to a peak

The day laid bare

Stripped to the bone

ROADBLOCK 4 *(I Am the Threshold)*

I am the threshold

Without dimension
Without comfort
Here is my other self
Made to stand on its toes

While writing the character for 'grave' (墓)
I detect the smell of 'India ink' (墨)
Or it seems that way, I'm sure of it
My other self
The one who dances

Between stalks of white horseweed
How far … how far
Stretching all the way to the end of summer
The train tracks rusted red

Look
One threshold overlaps another
When held, there are any number of places you can rest
O dancing one
Fragments of sparkling faces fall
All along the furrow of your spine

Like a benediction

And when it falls on me
O dancing one
You have already departed silently from the threshold
And again from somewhere
The smell of India ink

The threshold
Diligently mixes the murmur of voices with hushed silence

It's only me
The threshold …

Parade 5

The day laid bare

Actions take hold of the human and then pass away with frightening speed

Or a passage through hell
What fun

TWENTY-THIRD FLESH is a mystery. It's all been packed away. (If you close your eyes you can see the buildings collapse one after the other.)

TWENTY-FOURTH FLESH – if we considered for a moment the possibility that it has something we might call spirit, it would crawl slowly through the depths of the abyss, and begin licking something like the organic whispers which have collected on top of the sludge of time. Essentially a gelatinous substance, all of its pigment has drained off.

TWENTY-FIFTH FLESH wears the expression of an idiot even if abused, or more precisely, it has regenerated many times over still wearing the same expression. If you chop it up into a thousand fragments, each one of those thousand particles will likely regenerate itself.

Because it is equal to the fate of the breast

Metallic moss grows near the water's edge
Exposed to irradiation from an intense light
All …
All is laid bare

TWENTY-SIXTH FLESH is difficult to describe. It seems to have gotten the hang of this game called existence with incredible speed, but ...

Forgive me

Beside your dry slumber

We'll set aside **TWENTY-SEVENTH FLESH** for the moment. It can take care of itself. Capable of holding up under almost any kind of burden, its metabolic rate is perfectly steady. It'll live to be a hundred, but the land promised it is miniscule.

'Welcome to the oasis of true love,' says **TWENTY-EIGHTH FLESH**, but it keeps its clothes on. It's not a question of technique, or of sexual difference. It's just that its whole digestion process goes on in plain sight. How about finding a way to make your internal organs look smaller ...

Over-calculated, over-managed

At the water's edge

The shining of a light too intense
For love

ROADBLOCK 5 *(The Zone)*

I am immersed
In the zone
You are immersed in the chill waters
In the depths of my brain
Water like mercury

A bloody head, a head like a honey white peach
Emerges from between a woman's legs
I try to push it back

From the right jawbone
Of my death mask
The face of a misshapen infant appears
Screaming, howling

Love is a tornado of hunger and thirst, bearing the rawness of
the zone
existence from breath to breath, and at the same time a cau-
tionary note regarding the birds which pass through the tornado
the zone
like areolae.

Zone
Zone
You in your nakedness
I become immersed in you
You of the soft, ample, swelling flesh
In the depths of my brain
A tin bathtub overflowing
Bitter cold water like mercury

I push the honey white peach
And shout
Don't come out! Birth is disaster! Misfortune!
I try to push it back
Back into the cave-like darkness of the woman
Hands covered in blood

Stop! Please stop!
My own and only death mask is enough!
But my cries are useless
The infant's face comes, gradually appears
Becomes more and more distorted
Its nose and other features crushed

Love is the banner of unwashed flesh[the zone] breathing, dancing on a fragment of silk from the sea. And it is the blemish on the demented white voice advancing as if to caress[the zone] the other side of breathing.

Birth is disaster

Birth is misfortune

Zone
Zone
Zone
You are Venus, Venus returned to water

Now the face of the infant
Occupies nearly the entire lower half
Of the right jawbone of my death mask
And advances on the bridge of the nose

Love is the mapping of the seminal emission of this or that
the zone
person, as it is sprayed into the embryo of death's panting. And
it is the slow ballad of the rainbow, which is a joke but is required
for mapping.

> A brutal struggle ensues between
> The head, trying to come out
> And myself trying to push it back
> The woman's crotch becomes an arena

Zone
I kill you with an electrical charge
Zone
I kill you by stuffing you with gravel

> My death mask it must be somewhere in the frontal region
> Breaks open and the hippocampus splatters everywhere
> Then someone crams a test tube in there
> Making a squeaking sound

the zone
Love is individual sea slugs of intoxication which continue as if
stitching together the skin's winter. And it is the dark buzzing of
the zone
flies as they pass through decorating each one of them.

> Collapse of the honey white peach
> The apocalyptic text written in blood and milk

Zone
You no longer speak
Your body is colder than water

So I cram in plenty of letters
    The riddle of the test tube, the squeaking sound
    Somebody…

Love is …

PARADE 6

Look – it's happening again
Humans possessed
By actions

Oh merciful Buddha (The collarbone snaps)

One continues to practice self-restraint

I whisper to you, the winter of your skin exfoliates

Look –

Another parade. **TWENTY-NINTH FLESH** comes into view. Its peculiar mode of existence is like the hallucinations when some bad stuff kicks in. That's how much it shakes its head as if it had been severed, twirling around in an absurd dance. If you ever manage to capture it, you will notice a strong smell of citrus.

Shaking its head as if it had been severed

(Read the writing on the wall JAPAN)

THIRTIETH FLESH is a balloon swollen with the ashes of existence, or the carrier of ardor's return. When desire is fulfilled it flattens, and then waits for more ashes. It will wait years if necessary.

And at the far end of its ordeal
Yet again it sucks, sucks and absorbs

THIRTY-FIRST FLESH unfolds its solitude like fins at rest. Radiating outward, with delicacy; to pursue or be pursued; such concepts simply rain down like marine snow.

Before talking about **THIRTY-SECOND FLESH** it's back down memory lane – the movie *Alien*, nostalgiasville! My precious little alien, shuffling around the attic, carrying off grandmother and the others, spinning them into cocoons …

Things have cleared up now, for us and the ground also
The egg and loneliness, an IV and a gag
See, it's all clear

The day laid bare

Because it is equal to the fate of the breast

Roadblock 6 *(Unknown Skin)*

1. PRECURSOR

No doubt it was late on a languid afternoon when my fingers crept along your lower abdomen toward the area where the pubic hairs begin to grow. I was just thinking, *almost there to the long-awaited genitals*, when without warning your lower abdomen changed into the wall of a dilapidated hospital. The shadow of an IV tube swung back and forth, then words appeared there in the form of graffiti, saying 'Return me to my natural state, I who have been born deformed.' Then before long the wall itself began to transform …

2. THE PURE SKIN TREATMENT SCHEME

Unknown skin

    Unknown
Skin

      Calm, peaceful
            Ashen husks
                As if numb from cold
            Doing the Hula

Sleepless flesh – look
            Uh-huh?
            Suspend the brain
        Expose (root)
            Earth Mother-ing
      Letter-weed-ing

Tomorrow's left and right
                    Placed against inner leaf

                        Wheat bran
                Faint-
                        ly
                        Centralized
            Tiny bubbles mixed in

                    Oops
        The innards
                    Embossed
        Edge of
        Weave
                    Zory
                    Ory
    Sweat glistening
                    The whole of
        To breathe in
                    Deeply
        And trem
                    ble

                    Unknown
        Skin
    Unknown skin

Like
A long-awaited
Shore

At some point
It gathers
Unknown skin

Unknown
Skin

Moving toward it
Gradually
We stop naming things

After all, if you touch them
They become exactly
What they are – a leaf
Or a stem, etc. etc.

Ah, finger nails, half moon
Drool
Someone (embarks
For the floating world)
Do not call it either male or female

But
For some people
The person is formed by moving ever closer to nature – the
        non-human
There are a certain number of people like this

The skin
Its scent
Appearing as the layers are peeled away
Peeling away, appearing, only then reaching
The unknown

Even so
There's not a chance we would actually become like that
Rather, we encounter it through touch
Or abandonment
Which leads us there

Scent
Of skin
Unknown

Dappled in sunlight
One narrowly manages (to embark
For the floating world) with several wounds
Now the wounds open

Gathering
Unknown skin
Unknown
Skin

I am searching for a hiragana woman
A woman who wants to become a hiragana character ... or so
    she says
Somehow I understand. After all, I myself
Have a dislike for the kanji character 'man' (男). The least they
    could do
Is spell it out using the alphabet. So while thinking this
I go in search of a hiragana woman
Kisaragi, Yayoi – oh whatever could it be
The skin's gathering, in which there is no clearing up

Or is it like day and night, or somewhere in the void between
    them
Into which she enters, having determined precisely the right
    timing
The woman, simply because she is syllabic,
Is not necessarily old fashioned – from between jeans and T-shirt
Her belly button peers out
Only to become a hiragana character

Let's break it down for a closer look, what's it all about
Both body and soul get all sudsy
Adrift in the world like lint, or, I wonder ...
Beneath that drifting do long, slender fingers appear
Like the gentle hand of the Bodhisattva?
I don't know, I wonder
So I go along mumbling these words (I really don't know)
While seeking the hiragana woman

There are kittens, and soap lathering up
And in the dim light I notice
How I am entangled in the overgrown tendrils of my own desire
Something like the sadness of living things

But hey, the hiragana woman
Is a more distant conclusion, of which we cannot speak
Possibly approaching a person's last breath, the essential
So I delay the timing and again make my entrance
But what should I do if I should find her?

When you think about what it takes to make woman (女) or
      wife (妻)
And how many strokes are required, it just gets to be a pain
      in the neck
Shimotsuki, shiwasu – whatever could it be
The skin, whose lack of clarity
Like dim light crushed or pressed, like idleness or vacuity
This gathering in which, yes, I also
Would like to blend in, would like to end it all

Stripped to the bone

All is laid bare

Go, follow – give chase

THIRTY-THIRD FLESH laughs, laughs as if its open mouth had grown naturally right out of the surface of the earth. Soon a shaft of light will hit this blatantly nonsensical life form.

THIRTY-FOURTH FLESH – just what is this? Talk about the consequences of evolution … it has the spirit of a huge cyclopean eye and nerves like a high-tech alloy fiber. But unfortunately, it's weak-kneed like literature.

THIRTY-FIFTH FLESH is equipped with strength, speed, and ferocity – so much so it's almost embarrassing. But its face is calm … there must be some kind of mistake.

With the scent of your long hair
This life of yours in the fast lane accelerates

Accept your limitations
Or be eaten alive

Thus **THIRTY-FIFTH FLESH** torments **TWENTY-SEVENTH FLESH** without interruption until it progresses to **THIRTY-SIXTH FLESH**. Then **THIRTY-THIRD FLESH** provides unwavering support to **TWENTY-NINTH FLESH** until it advances to **THIRTY-SEVENTH FLESH**. **TWENTY-SECOND FLESH** hurriedly tramples over **TWENTY-FIFTH FLESH** and remains in the twenty-second spot to this day.

THIRTY-EIGHTH FLESH is surprisingly long. It takes in the sand and sludge of the spirit and filters out trace amounts of inspiration. With only that much to feed off of, it's amazing how it's able to cover its energy needs. The key word just may be suspended animation (or apparent death)

Mr Goosebumps

War or micro-war
On the front cover of the dream
Begins to spread faintly like bleeding under the skin

THIRTY-NINTH FLESH is also surprisingly long. When you touch it, it shrinks, and if you take hold of it, it coils itself around your hand. Every now and then it has intense convulsions like a medium in a trance.

FORTIETH FLESH is in such a hurry, it barely takes time to say hello. So what's the rush?

FORTY-FIRST FLESH speaks: 'You who live on the surface, come down! Come down to these depths. It is good here in the deep. You can get by on low metabolism, and when friends drop by from time to time, you can open your big stupid mouth and swallow them up.'

Lo and behold, **FORTY-SECOND FLESH** is nearly all light, or the semblance of a life lived sending minute ripples to beat against fine, luminous hairs. Somehow deep inside of Venus ...

How stupid, it's certainly not a neon sign on a pachinko parlor.

Go in pursuit of unknown flesh, of the disappeared

ROADBLOCK 7 *(Submerge Your Face)*

Submerge! (Be joyful!
Your face (the afternoon also
In the depths of the brain (it's the brain

Be joyful!
The afternoon also is brain
The name for meditation (the name of enlightenment
We (we are inside your brain
Your face (your own face (is submerged in the depths of
        the brain
Gently (as if to care for (in advance of
Like burial (it is our small selves (the workings of
        something greater
Because (at the depths of the brain (strangely sticky water
        (all day long
Is praised (there it is submerged (the face (to the farthest
        depths the face
And by the wristwatches and stuff (your passport and so on
And even the rose-colored sand you brought back with you
        from the Sahara
Yes (like items buried with the dead (at which point soon
        (the name of enlightenment
The name of rapture (we (we in sticky water
The face (our faces which were to have been submerged
        (their slow emergence from the depths
We look at them (they are like granules of mercury (submit
        to the froth of words
Cool and crisp (a bit swollen (altogether like a different person
Like a baboon (like Jupiter (be joyful!
It is the brain of afternoon (of the lovely
Afternoon of brain

Be joyful! (Submerge!
Afternoon also (the face
The brain (in the depths of the brain

Parade 8

Stripped to the bone

The grasslands continue on in the distance
Ground of unraveling sutures

Go, follow – give chase

It's a parade. **FORTY-THIRD FLESH** appears. It's one great big mouth, and yet it is capable of running. Call it 'the running mouth' – Running Mouth!

FORTY-FOURTH FLESH is myself.

Monitored, scanned

'Received passionate love letters from Miyuki, and e-mails expressing sweet nothings ... how was I to know it was a trap, that it meant death? I was taken for all I had.'

A prayer, ever so faintly a prayer
Is woven into a fabric
Moving along the faint trepidation of life

FORTY-FIFTH FLESH – is this also myself? Braving poison thorns of the external world or that which is named world to bite down hard, bringing it into the interior and transporting it to the vibrating back-end, making it into one's own defense weapon ...

How brave ...

FORTY-SIXTH FLESH knows. That an infallible defense mechanism does not exist, while being completely absorbed in looking almost like a kind of seaweed.

JAPAN –

Here and there, like pockmarks, there are bases of another country, as if it were a protectorate.

FORTY-SEVENTH FLESH has an interior shaped like an uncanny lump, or a lump shaped like an interior. Why does it carry around such a useless thing? It doesn't exactly attract the opposite sex, and it's not packed with nutrients. It clearly operates in an adverse manner when it comes to survival.

Color is clearly the major characteristic of **FORTY-EIGHTH FLESH**, but those colors instantaneously transform before our very eyes, leaving us in dismay.

Now look at **FORTY-NINTH FLESH**, but before that look at **FORTY-FIFTH FLESH** and **FORTY-SIXTH FLESH**. We can say nothing of them here. They can only become something else – something other than themselves.

Secretly
Adenylic acid
Guanylic acid

ROADBLOCK 8 *(Between Waking and Sleep)*

Between waking and sleep
You embark
On the day of absence
How
Could you have known
You would become a corpse
Only hours later
The sky taking on a tinge of blue at daybreak
A pale moon hanging there
Like a broken-off piece of bone
Shot through with small holes and cracks
As if only there could time ripen

Oh momentous
Egg
Pitching a tent

Between waking and sleep
I too eventually arrive
Day of
Nothingness
A thin cold layer
So that the phantom city may break free of shadows
Rising, lips pursed
A festival of voices
First, breathlessly scattering storm seeds
Then, as if dancing slowly, gently
Around the edge of the moon
Whose voice travels
The melancholy voice
Splitting into several strands
Each whimsically formed into flesh and bone

The phantom city opens its town square
And there the voices
Flesh of voices, bone of voices
Come flooding into the square like a torrent of light
Now all manner of invocation, myriads of prayers
Are called into being
Even atonement ascends the pavement
Of enthusiasm
And when they become innumerable banners and begin
       to flutter
I also will move along the rim of solidarity
Eyes penetrating
The will
Ears shattering the silence

No
No, not like that
To accept the bewilderment of the unknown
Into the furthest reaches of the nervous system
And while still excited
Disappear

PARADE 9

How colorful –
Cytidylic acid
Thymidylic acid

FIFTIETH FLESH is like a fish which has passed out, startled by a shock wave. Or if not, the only way left to describe it would be that it's like an anus. If possible, we would like to return to the mouth, that essential passage without which utterance or the act of eating would be impossible. But it has neither a large or small intestine, nor even a stomach. It lacks that very organ through which things must pass in order to return to the mouth. Even so, why is it that adults always seem to forget completely about their own childhood?

Or so it seems

Ground of unraveling sutures

Language
Sneaks in through the back door of tactile perception

In speaking of **FIFTY-FIRST FLESH**, one gets the feeling that one must take into consideration manner of meeting, safety guarantee, coexistence, physical relationship, and many other factors. In other words, there is the sense that without speaking of virtually every possible thing which could be spoken of, it will not be possible to speak at all.

Then in the midst of entertaining doubts **FIFTY-SECOND FLESH** goes under, or you could say it forms an image of itself sinking and gets drunk on that image.

For example a stone sinks down into the depths of the brain, then another stone sinks down after it, then another and another, numerous stones following.

Then **FIFTY-THIRD FLESH** sinks also,

Sinks down until it reaches a certain type of skin which is more expansive, or toward a crepuscular light called *human* …

A prayer, ever so faintly a prayer

Monitored, scanned

Because it is equal to the fate of the breast

FIFTY-FOURTH FLESH is a *Pipa pipa*, oh merciful Buddha a *Pipa pipa*, and a laugh with many folds and creases which, if unfurled, would provide a spread the size of a tennis court's redemption.

Obligation to provide disclosure; anonymity of mutual back-
    scratching
Just a little madness

ROADBLOCK 9 *(One, Two ...)*

It's hot (there's no time (in the vicinity of the last day
Reeds of light come streaming through
Something more (something broken or missing
Let's count them (the days and the nights
Until you can sleep no more

One (two
One (two

Let us follow the rallying cry
From dogs' excrement (it will fall (behind the medical center

While it's still soft (this body
Ash mixes with blood
A wedge harasses the voice
This body
Walnuts low price or gratis (there's no time
Footsteps (like a refined rhinoceros

Something more
Destined to become lost
When it's fragrant we close shop (fi ... (fighting spirit (fiber
At its apex (sexual organs or entrails are preferred
The face is, like, yuck
Let us count again

One (two
One (two

Hot (reeds of light come streaming through
Ah, how far
The face is, like, yuck (the sound of leaves rustling
Sexual organs or entrails preferred

Parade 10

Singularity of nakedness
Splendor of gravitational force

'We perform somersaults while remaining connected doggy style'

It's a parade. **FIFTY-FIFTH FLESH** emanates light – light like human excrement, like voices of anger, like faces weeping.

FIFTY-SIXTH FLESH transforms itself into all manner of things, one after the other. At one moment it is the sexual love of an octopus, and yet another, contemplation like a jellyfish. Once, it shifts into reboot like a stingray because in a naked, sandy place with nowhere to hide (in other words, what we call existence), it is especially dangerous to retain the same form.

FIFTY-SEVENTH FLESH is like a free-floating shellfish, or possibly something like the phantasmagoric shape of a flying tortoise. More precisely, it is a fetus. A fetus which walks from belly to belly, poaching unknown ferocious mutant organisms in the sea.

Thus you must love it
Like a spring bursting open uncharacteristically

Oh river of curtains floating downstream, oh ridicule on record,
     oh leisure of eddies
The reason you were called upon remains obscure
Smothered in DNA, oh shock wave exposed, oh first embankment

FIFTY-EIGHTH FLESH has met with apparent death, and is filled with screams. In the midst of this a face, a face which cannot quite be called a face, climbs from the abdominal region to the chest. Then it struggles desperately to crawl from there to the top of the neck.

Filled with apparent death, filled with screams

When all is said and done, it seems an ominous prelude to disaster

War or micro-war
'It has come for you'

There is no place left

FIFTY-NINTH FLESH translates, or is translated. 'I skin you, I door you, so you bone me and chutzpah me, then comet me.'

Just like identifying an area for computer terminals

SIXTIETH FLESH has almost nothing of what one might call thickness. First showing its back side then its front, the exquisite angle and movement of its easy swaying back and forth is like a dried leaf sinking in water.

SIXTY-FIRST FLESH or massacre in the blink of an eye – whether perpetrator or victim, a blink in the moment of massacre …

SIXTY-SECOND FLESH is a misshapen reactor in which scraps of spirit repeat indefinitely moments of cooling and explosion. The protective wall that surrounds it, and the toxic gas, neither of which is tolerable …

Come, come my captor

'Half-naked I flee'

Roadblock 10 (Shadow of Flesh)

You, shined on by sun, and above
Shadow of flesh swaying
It is myself …
What have I become?
A shadow wandering
Expanding, contracting
Changing shape like an amoeba
Swaying back and forth
Yes, it's me
An old song wafts in on the breeze
Might be Lenny Kravitz
'Are You Gonna Go My Way?'
More and more the shadow moves
Dances to the beat of the music
But it is not having fun
Simply becomes more and more the shadow
The shadow which
Above you, on whom the sun shines,
Begins to go mad, as if flipping to the beat
Heading in no direction, resembling a prayer
It is myself
Shined on by never-ending sun
Floating endlessly above you

Please, somebody – skin me, door me, bone me
I will chutzpah you and comet you

And then …

The leveling down

SIXTY-THIRD FLESH is able to turn itself inside out. It transforms itself into something like a sea urchin, repositioning its thorns normally located deep inside so that they face outward for protection. Come, come my captor, even your thoughts are released from your head.

On the back of the spirit possessed by **SIXTY-FOURTH FLESH**, its shadow swells like a brightly-colored tattoo.

SIXTY-FIFTH FLESH is extremely small and fragile, so much so that merely touching it will cause it to break. There's no telling when it lost its shell, but in its place, it disgorges a netting of mucoid words which it spreads like wings. How beautiful. The only time it can rest its wings is when it unites with the sludge oozing from the depths of nonbeing.

Thus the death of **FIFTY-NINTH FLESH** is the life of **FIFTY-FOURTH FLESH**, while the prognosis of **FORTY-EIGHTH FLESH** is the precursor of **FIFTY-FIRST FLESH**, but that's all water under the bridge.

Do not forget – the withered sea slug
The poaching fetuses, and the midnight attraction of squirming

SIXTY-SIXTH FLESH is literally spineless. It manages to come up with a slippery smile and then takes the place of **SIXTY-SEVENTH FLESH**. Then it moves on to the position of **SIXTY-EIGHTH FLESH** without shedding blood despite getting its skin cut. Using a modified version of the door to the past, it advances to the place of **SIXTY-NINTH FLESH**, and then while multiplying the number of gelatinous umbrellas, it takes on the position of **SEVENTIETH FLESH**.

And then the trembling, the trembling like convulsions, races around this circle of flesh. Or flesh comes into communication with trembling, the convulsion-like trembling.

SEVENTY-FIRST FLESH bounces around, a tremendous bouncing, which continues ad nauseam until the point it comes to be called leaf of the spirit.

SEVENTY-SECOND FLESH is not fleshy at all. It has lost all substance, living only as a pair of phantom legs. But they are an elegant pair of legs, likely holding both sexuality and thought within.

SEVENTY-THIRD FLESH stands guard, or is about to instigate a riot.

Shaking its head as if it had none – yes, yes that's it, as if re-membering, shaking one's head as if headless ...

Light
Voice

SEVENTY-FOURTH FLESH is deflated ... I place my mouth over the hole open in the abdominal region and feed air into it. Now it will become swollen again, perhaps fall in love again ...

Doona Bae
Doona Bae

May fall in love
As the saying goes, with spirit and so on

ROADBLOCK 11 *(Separation)*

I. TWITTERING OF BIRDS WHICH TRANSCENDS BIRDS

Space
Space is the question
The in-between
The interval
Separation
Twittering
Twittering of birds which transcends birds
Or a shriek
Above a shallow ravine
Waving in the breeze like long hair, a shriek undulating
Or encircling
Encircling of breath, which is also the threshold where breath
       is cut off
Or an image
The elements laid bare are
An image of the unexpurgated real running rampant like a
       tiny Venus
Its smooth
Rim carrying
The engraving of roughly drawn letters
Separation
Who was it again?
Who was I supposed to be?

2. LU-LI-LI

Space
Space is the question
The in-between
The interval
Snow and breath
Star and eye
Have an in-between
Empty place
In-between place
Sepa—ration
In purple rhythms
First prop up a pillar
Then bend the sky like a ring
Insect
Insect of ecstasy
Make it run
Lu-li-li
Li-li
When the corridor called the chain of whispers comes into being
A hollow sound
A beam
It is the city's beginning, city of nesting and procreation
Of gathering …
For scenery
An aurora is thrown in
The boundaries of people's skin are dispersed

Extends even into the voice –

The naked day

Go, follow – give chase

It's another parade. **SEVENTY-FIFTH FLESH** now comes into view. It is a nocturnal beast, and moves like a ghost through the shadows of your brain. When its probing detects a potato bug in your dreams, it plunges its outlandishly long hooks inside, digs the worm out and devours it with pleasure.

SEVENTY-SIXTH FLESH has spots, or has gotten annoyingly preachy, or is difficult to touch, or is something like a spiral, or perhaps is like a toe thinking about world affairs.

SEVENTY-SEVENTH FLESH has eight rings, or six rings, and brings with it the classical term for land, in hopes of hatching the slimy **SEVENTY-EIGHTH FLESH** from there.

Let's see now ... what was that line?
The sacred cluster of rocks

SEVENTY-NINTH FLESH – when captured, its lustrous voice is cut out and its body discarded, after which it eventually dies.

EIGHTIETH FLESH exudes a net consisting of massive amounts of mucus from its body, which reminds one of a penis, or it may really be just a penis.

Extends even into the voice

EIGHTY-FIRST FLESH, whose luminous pouch you find to be so undignified, just may in fact be yourself.

EIGHTY-SECOND FLESH mimics the others to the extent that it has become excessive. For instance, if one of these others happens to be you, how do we know where you begin and end? Such an uncanny resemblance …

EIGHTY-THIRD FLESH – the male of the species gives birth to its young, receiving the egg shapes from the female in a dream, and sheltering them in his head. Then in due course, the tiny babies are discharged.

Crowds overflowing with sexuality
Sexuality overflowing with crowds

EIGHTY-FOURTH FLESH secludes itself in its nest until it becomes one with the nest. Those who have accepted a life like that must be coaxed to spend at least one night of this imperfect existence and crawl out of their hovel as if possessed, indulging themselves in the mating dance, squirming and wriggling. *Sons-of-bitches dancing like crazy.*

EIGHTY-FIFTH FLESH lives a twisted life. It displays a mysterious phosphorescence whose true identity is unknown.

Now an intense light shines
On all things

EIGHTY-SIXTH FLESH, or an ear which has died of natural causes; **EIGHTY-SEVENTH FLESH**, or a tongue which has died of natural causes; **EIGHTY-EIGHTH FLESH**, or morning sickness which has died of natural causes; **EIGHTY-NINTH FLESH**, or an aura which has died of natural causes.

So what are you calling fun? Like a group of ghosts, these embodiments become wisps of smoke wafting on the breeze, an intense light shining through each one of them.

For **NINETIETH FLESH**, particularly for its swimming spirit, each day is exceedingly short, perhaps only three hours long. During those few hours it makes the complacency of mercury its own, makes the powerlessness of mercury its own.

Sons-of-bitches dancing like crazy

The sun star cometh

… maybe

NINETY-FIRST FLESH is, quite simply, always already the sun star which cometh, or so it seems. With tentacles that move at will and an epidermis soft as velvet, though it is blind it closes in, deftly avoiding all manner of obstacles.

At long last the sun star cometh
The sun star cometh

Nearly crushed beneath its weight, we begin to draw our own elegant line of flight.

Go, follow – give chase

ROADBLOCK 12 *(Cockscomb Cockscomb)*

Cockscombs –
Must be at least fourteen or fifteen of them
End of song
By way of
An interior wind which throws its clothes aside, we who are
　　pseudo-embodiments
Like a reprieve
Swaying
Or reprieve like an eel wriggling, its shadow cut off
An ending like a reprieve
The chill
At the rim of death
And yet cockscombs –
Must be at least fourteen or fifteen cockscombs
Fourteen or fifteen there are
There must be
Fourteen or fifteen of which I see
There must be, this illness which I have gained, unable to
　　crawl out of bed, I
Can only look at these fourteen or fifteen flowers at the far
　　end of the garden
Deep in the garden
Oh sister my sister
That light there must be an insect, insects also
Must be gelatin the garden in back
Cockscomb's cockscombs
Fourteen or fifteen there must be
Empty, vain yet beautiful this flesh, its final breath
Like blood overflowing
Like letters
Like hair like thread
Or people

So people must be threads winding where thread is gelatin
Must be the far end of the garden where cockscombs
Peoplepeoplepeople
Wind in and out like vines, dancing, moving spasmodically
The fourteen flowers I see and am seen
We who are pseudo-embodiments
Oh sister
Does it exist, the winding in and out and dancing in the garden
The movements
Like
Spasms

PARADE 13

Go, follow – give chase
Otherwise you yourself will become a fugitive

Exposed

An intense light shines on all things
All is laid bare

NINETY-SECOND FLESH has an Amadeus organ, a Caravaggio organ, and a phoenix organ, so with this flesh on the outside, a large variety of heterogeneous velocities are channeled through it in order to convert it into primeval chaos … flowing, shedding tears.

Flowing, shedding tears

NINETY-THIRD FLESH unleashes its attack so slowly it's irritating. Hence you can only see it if you approach with a show of friendliness, or wait, it may actually be launching its attack with a feeling of friendliness.

NINETY-FOURTH FLESH is called *sasa* …

I have in fact researched a number of cases of *sasa* in my day – I am *sasa*, you also are *sasa*. With this peculiar name, something like a collective emergency exit of the body begins to whisper. You can gather together even as one, gather together as one and then be made love to for someone, swelling along with the moon, the zero of blood and signs sprouting … *sasa* you are *sasa*, *sasa* I am *sasa*.

NINETY-FIFTH FLESH is a flower basket, a beautifully, delicately woven flower basket. Occasionally a couple wanders in, never to return. They are condemned to spend the rest of their lives in a boring love paradise, shadows the shape of the basket's weave projected onto their skin.

NINETY-SIXTH FLESH knows nothing of elimination, nor does it know fear. It has no knowledge of interest rates, and yet it knows. That a doll's life depends on its face, and that humans were originally born when a hole opened up.

NINETY-SEVENTH FLESH is the return of **TWENTY-SIXTH FLESH**. Had enough? Yes, the return. Hence it is beyond description – nameless. The game of existence itself is swallowed whole at an outrageous speed.

Is this a kind of shaky dynamic equilibrium?

NINETY-EIGHTH FLESH is also a recurrence. It is the return of **FOURTEENTH FLESH** or **FORTY-NINTH FLESH**, or of some other flesh.

NINETY-NINTH FLESH, yes, now we arrive at **NINETY-NINTH FLESH**. It bares itself and dances the Bolero. Then one by one the others, **FIRST FLESH** and **FIFTH FLESH**, gather round. Then **SEVENTH FLESH**, **ELEVENTH FLESH** and **TWENTY-THIRD FLESH** … and so **NINTH FLESH** and **TWENTY-EIGHTH FLESH** and **FORTY-FIRST FLESH** and **FIFTY-SIXTH FLESH** also gather round. Then together they dance the Bolero, dance to the regular rhythms …

Or a call to riot
In JAPAN also
A call to riot

NINETY-NINTH FLESH, which occupies the center, begins to blush, and increases the intensity of its movement. Its state of rapture spreads to the flesh on the periphery and its movements intensify further until it is no longer visible to the naked eye.

It is a good sign, the periphery, a prominence

ONE HUNDREDTH FLESH – at long last, flapping its wings, becomes a disembodied spirit.
The gods seem to have taken a liking to it, like a glistening lepidopteran.

It is a good sign, around the mouth a mere trace, a fragment of midday skin takes wing.

And with this **HUNDRED-AND-FIRST FLESH** makes its entry – it's a parade …

Go, follow – give chase

NOTES

EPIGRAPH: The Gherasim Luca epigraph (*There is no place left in this world for poets*) is from Luca's suicide note. It reflects Nomura's concern with the loss of poetry's former status in Japanese culture. In addition, Nomura and Luca can be seen as sharing a certain sense of the grotesque and the absurd, while at the same time being dead serious. The 'flesh' parading through Nomura's work have something in common with the Surrealist art objects created by Luca in the 1930s.

PARADE 2: *Hunter x Hunter* – this Japanese manga is available online in English translation. Adenylic acid and guanylic acid are building blocks of DNA.

PARADE 3: The words for blood, knowledge, and ground used in the description of EIGHTH FLESH each share the same sound *(chi),* but are written with different characters (血、知、地). Cytidylic acid and thymidylic acid are components of RNA.

PARADE 4: The words translated here as 'male' and 'female' are *osu* and *mesu* (雄、雌), which refer to male and female animals. The phrase 'point of torsion' most likely refers to the shape of DNA – the double helix.

ROADBLOCK 4: The characters for 'grave' (墓) and 'India ink' or *sumi* (墨) both contain the earth radical (土) in their lower half. Hence the connection made here.

ROADBLOCK 5: The word 'namu' (南無) is from the phrase 'Namu Amidha Butsu' (南無阿弥陀仏). Originating in Sanskrit, it is a prayer or chant used primarily in populist Buddhist sects such as Jodo and Nichiren. Two possible translations of the complete phrase are, 'I entrust myself to the infinite light and infinite life', or 'Homage to the Buddha of Boundless Compassion and Wisdom.'

PARADE 6: The word used here for 'Japan' is the English word, written in the katakana script. This gives the reader the impression that what is being spoken of is Japan in the context of the international community or Japan as seen by other countries. It can also have a somewhat sarcastic ring to it, i.e. a way of not taking Japan as a nation very seriously or of poking fun at it.

ROADBLOCK 6: In this poem Nomura engages in language play at several levels at once – using made-up words, words having primarily a rhythmic or sound quality, and plays on meanings using both the written character and sound. There is also much irony and humor in this poem, with subtitles such as 'The Pure Skin Treatment Scheme', which is quite possibly a quote from an advertising leaflet.

On page 41, the 'hiragana woman' wants to become a character in the hiragana script, which is one of the two syllabic character sets used in Japanese. Hiragana was developed in the twelfth century specifically for the use of aristocratic women in the writing of letters and poems (the men wrote in classical Chinese). It is still experienced as being an essentially 'feminine' script. Moreover, Nomura makes use of the script in some unusual ways, such as using を (the direct object particle which stands between a noun and its verb) to represent the sound 'o' rather than お, the standard character for representing this sound. He does use kanji (Chinese characters) in this section of the poem, but only very occasionally.

Also on page 41, Kisaragi and Yayoi are place names with associations in classical literature, including the types of writings (diaries and waka, traditional Japanese poetry) which would often be written in hiragana. Nomura slips into the feminine voice here, using an exclamatory tag phrase associated specifically with feminine speech. (Japanese has a very clear delineation between masculine and feminine speech, each having their own specific vocabularies.)

The Bodhisattva (page 41) is Kannon (観音), sometimes referred to as the Goddess of Mercy in English, usually depicted in Buddhist statuary with long, slender fingers.

'When you think about what it takes to make woman (女) or wife (妻)' (page 42). The first lines of this last stanza have a double meaning. One is to make someone one's woman or one's wife, requiring many 'strokes' (with a sexual connotation), and the other meaning is to write kanji or Chinese characters requiring many strokes of the brush (the traditional writing tool). (As explained previously, the poem plays on the association of the hiragana syllabary with the feminine and is written mostly in hiragana except for these and a few other kanji characters.) The characters for woman (女) and wife (妻) are similar (the character for wife contains the character for woman in its lower half). It takes a number of lines to draw these characters hence 'many strokes are required.' *Shimotsuki, shiwasu* (霜月, 師走) are old names for the months of November and December which went out of use once Japan switched to the Gregorian calendar.

PARADE 8: Here again the English word 'Japan' is used, appearing in the Katakana script. 'Secretly' (page 49) translates the classical phrase, *himeyaka naru kana*. The ending *kana* is used in both haiku and tanka to denote an ending or full stop.

ROADBLOCK 8: 'Between waking and sleep' is a translation of *hansui* (半睡), meaning 'hypnapagogic', or causing wakefulness; preventing sleep. A state similar to that through which the mind passes when coming out of sleep.

PARADE 9: 'How colorful' translates the classical term, *adeyaka naru kana*, which again uses *kana* to denote an ending or full stop.

ROADBLOCK 9: 'One, two' – *hii, fuu* in Japanese according to the old way of counting used before the introduction of kanji from China via the Korean peninsula in the fourth century AD. Its use in a modern context has a somewhat whimsical sense about it, and more connection to the childhood world and the intimacy of the family than other forms of counting. The old counting system only goes up to ten.

'Refined rhinoceros' (page 54) is a pun in Japanese, both words containing the sound 'sai' – *bisai na sai*. 'Fighting spirit' (戦意) and fiber (繊維) (also page 54) are homonyms in Japanese, both pronounced *sen'i* but with different kanji. The beginning of the same line, 'When it's fragrant …' *(Fukuiku to tatamareru)* may be a play on words alluding to one of Japan's earliest Modernist avant-garde magazines called *Fukuikutaru Kafuyo* (Ah Fragrant Stoker).

PARADE 11: 'Leaf of the spirit' plays on the classical Japanese term for 'word' *(koto no ha)*, which literally means 'leaves of things'. Doona Bae is a popular Korean movie actress. In a recent film, she plays an inflatable doll which comes to life. In many of the movie's scenes she appears fully nude.

ROADBLOCK 11: Space, the in-between, interstices, are all terms used in an attempt to translate the concept of Ma (間), or 'negative space.' It is an important concept in the traditional arts from the classic Noh drama to brush painting, meaning the pause or moment of silence in the drama, and the empty space in painting, which acts as an active or full space. The concept of Ma takes on a new level of importance in twentieth-century Japanese philosophy which, though heavily influenced by Western philosophy, begins to make use of certain native concepts by the 1930s. It is here that Ma takes on a new relationship with Bergson's 'duration'. The Japanese were deeply interested in Heidegger's thought as well, but rather than 'Being and Time', their interest was more in being and space. During the postwar period, we find artists involved in avant-garde performance, such as the Butoh dance, beginning to make use of the concept of Ma. Nomura's poem makes use of word play, especially sound and rhythm, returning regularly to the open vowel 'ah' which brings an especially lyric feel to this section of the poem (impossible to reproduce in translation) while at the same time engaging with the concept of space itself.

PARADE 12: The classical phrase quoted in Nomura's original is from the *Man'yōshū*, Japan's oldest poetry anthology compiled some time after 759 AD. It is written in an earlier form of the language using Chinese characters for their sound quality alone. Translator Matt Treyvaud renders it thus: 'In the river / the sacred clustered rocks / do not sprout grass / Would that [you] were ever thus – / an eternal maiden.' I have borrowed Treyvaud's translation of the line Nomura quotes, with just a minor change. This section of the poem also makes use of some obscure slang, for instance *hajiketa*, which would normally be translated as 'burst', means 'dance like crazy' or 'lose all self-consciousness'. The line 'The sun star cometh' makes use of *bungotai,* an archaic literary form. A sun star is a kind of star fish. Two lines later, the phrase 'line of flight' comes from the philosophy of Gilles Deleuze. This is a concept which was used in his work with Felix Guattari in *A Thousand Plateaus.* Nomura is the author of a book on Rimbaud in which he offers an interpretation of the poet's works from a Deleuzean perspective.

ROADBLOCK 12: The opening lines of this section of the poem paraphrase a famous haiku by Masaoka Shiki: 'Cockscombs – / I'm sure there are at least / fourteen or fifteen stalks (translated by Donald Keene). The Japanese reads *Keitoh no juushigohon mo arinubeshi*. A cockscomb (or plumed cockscomb) is a flower (*Celosia argentea*). Shiki wrote this poem during the last months of his life. While sick in bed he gazed out at the garden, and could see the flowers from there. Nomura's poem adopts the entire background of this haiku, referring also to Shiki's illness (apparently the speaker of the poem is Shiki himself, 'at the rim of death').

PARADE 13: *Sasa* is used here for its sound and rhythmical value. It is also a kind of bamboo grass. In the phrase 'a call to riot' (*boudou no susume*) on page 71, the word *susume* means basically a recommendation, although it can be used to advocate something. The phrase also is an ironic comment on one of the most well-known and important works produced at the beginning of Japan's race to modernization at the end of the nineteenth century – *Gakumon no Susume* (On Education) by Fukuzawa Yuukichi. The word *boudou* means insurrection, or uprising, as well as riot. Here again, Nomura uses the English word for 'Japan,' spelled out in the katakana syllabary, rather than the Japanese word. On page 72 Nomura uses the English word 'prominence', though written in katakana. A prominence is a large, bright, gaseous feature extending outward from the Sun's surface, often in a loop shape. A lepidopteran is a member of the classification *Lepidoptera*, an order of insects including moths and butterflies. One of the most obvious characteristics shared by members of this order is scales covering their bodies and wings.

The Author

Kiwao Nomura, who was born in 1951, is the leading experimental voice in contemporary Japanese poetry. He is also a major critic and theorist, who, along with Shuri Kido, has been responsible for providing a whole new interpretation of Japan's postwar period in literature. He has also written on French poets, including a book-length analysis of Rimbaud as seen through the concepts of Deleuze and Guattari. He has published twenty-six volumes of verse since 1987. A selected poems in English translation, *Spectacle and Pigsty: Selected Poems of Kiwao Nomura*, translated by Kyoko Yoshida and Forrest Gander, was published in the US by Omnidawn in 2011; this translation of *The Day Laid Bare*, originally published in Japanese in 2011, is the first time one of his individual volumes has been translated into English. In September 2020 the Japan Poets Association awarded him the 38th Modern Poetry Prize for his 2019 volume *Twilight Saudade*.

The Translator

Eric Selland has been translating Modernist and contemporary Japanese poets for nearly forty years, with works appearing in a variety of journals and anthologies. He has also published articles on Japanese Modernist poetry and translation theory. His latest collection of poems is *Object States* (Theenk Books, 2018). Other recent books are *Arc Tangent* (Isobar Press, 2013), and *Beethoven's Dream* (Isobar Press, 2015). Eric has also translated a number of contemporary novels, including *The Guest Cat*, by Takashi Hiraide, published by New Directions in the US and Picador in the UK, which was on both the *New York Times* and the UK *Sunday Times* bestseller lists in 2014. Eric lives in Tokyo with his wife and a black Shiba Inu named Ku.

Lightning Source UK Ltd.
Milton Keynes UK
UKHW012028161020
371722UK00001B/26